I0814130

UNDERSTANDING YOU

UNDERSTANDING INTEGRITY

by Elizabeth Andrews

Cody Koala
An Imprint of Pop!
popbooksonline.com

abdobooks.com
Published by Pop!, a division of ABDO, PO Box 398166, Minneapolis, Minnesota 55439.

Cody Koala™ is a trademark and logo of Pop!.

Printed in the United States of America, North Mankato, Minnesota

052022
092022

THIS BOOK CONTAINS RECYCLED MATERIALS

Cover Photo: Shutterstock Images
Interior Photos: Shutterstock Images, GettyImages

Editor: Grace Hansen
Series Designer: Victoria Bates

Library of Congress Control Number: 2021951837

Publisher's Cataloging-in-Publication Data
Names: Andrews, Elizabeth, author.
Title: Understanding integrity / by Elizabeth Andrews
Description: Minneapolis, Minnesota : Pop, 2023 | Series: Understanding you | Includes online resources and index
Identifiers: ISBN 9781098242152 (lib. bdg.) | ISBN 9781644948514 (pbk.) | ISBN 9781098242855 (ebook)
Subjects: LCSH: Integrity--Juvenile literature. | Feelings--Juvenile literature. | Social interaction--Juvenile literature. | Interpersonal relations--Juvenile literature.
Classification: DDC 152.4--dc23

Hello! My name is

Cody Koala

Pop open this book and you'll find QR codes like this one, loaded with information, so you can learn even more!

Scan this code* and others like it while you read, or visit the website below to make this book pop.

popbooksonline.com/integrity

*Scanning QR codes requires a web-enabled smart device with a QR code reader app and a camera.

Table of Contents

Chapter 1

Guidelines for Living

A person with integrity has strong **morals**. This means they know what is right and wrong. A moral person will always try their best to make the right choices.

Watch a video here!

Each person has their own set of morals. People can think different things are right and wrong. Children might learn morals from family members, school, books, friends, or **religion**.

Choosing to treat others the way you want to be treated is an example of a moral.

Bailey knows that it is important to be kind to everyone. Her grandma taught her that. Bailey invites her new classmate to play with her at recess. She knows it's hard to meet new friends.

Chapter 2

When No One Is Looking

Integrity means doing the right thing even when no one is looking. Some people want credit for the good deeds they do. They are doing the right thing for **selfish** reasons, not **moral** reasons.

Children with integrity will take only one piece of candy.

While Hannah is walking her dog in the park, she sees someone ahead of her drop their empty pop bottle on the ground. Hannah picks up the bottle and puts it in the next recycling bin she sees.

Chapter 3

Someone to Trust

People who have integrity are trustworthy. When they say they are going to do something, you can count on them to do it.

People with integrity only make promises they know they can keep.

Explore links here!

Nolan and Ezra borrow their parents' phones for the afternoon to play games. They each give them back when they get home for dinner.

Chapter 4

How to Act with Integrity

People with integrity will say "please" and "thank you." They will ask how they can help. They will stand up for people who are being treated poorly.

Complete an activity here!

To have integrity, you need to be honest and fair. It is a good **quality** for people to have. Having integrity makes a person a good member of the community.

Good leaders, like teachers and principals, act with integrity.

Making Connections

Text-to-Self

Can you think of any morals you have? Where or who did you learn them from?

Text-to-Text

Have you read any other books about being a good person? What do they have in common with this one?

Text-to-World

Do you think the world would be better or worse if everyone acted with integrity? Explain your answer.

Glossary

morals – ideas or habits of behavior that relate to what is right and what is wrong.

quality – something that makes a person who they are.

religion – a set of beliefs and rules used to honor a god or gods.

selfish – overly concerned with oneself.

Index

Online Resources

popbooksonline.com

Thanks for reading this Cody Koala book!

Scan this code* and others like it in this book, or visit the website below to make this book pop!

popbooksonline.com/integrity

*Scanning QR codes requires a web-enabled smart device with a QR code reader app and a camera.